The Glory of
the Cross

The Glory of the Cross

Gwynn Williams

*The substance of addresses originally given in Welsh
under the title 'In the cross of Christ I glory'*

BRYNTIRION PRESS

Biblical quotations are taken from the British usage text of
The Holy Bible, New King James Version
© Thomas Nelson, Inc., 1982

Cover design: Creative Media Publishing Limited

These addresses were first published in Welsh (Bryntirion Press, 2008)
under the title *Croes fy Arglwydd*, which is available from the publishers.

Bryntirion Press is grateful to Heath Evangelical Church, Cardiff,
for their support for this title.

Published by Bryntirion Press, Bryntirion, Bridgend CF31 4DX, Wales
Printed in Wales by Gomer Press, Llandysul

In memory of my father, the
Revd J. D. Williams, Ammanford

Contents

Contents

Preface

IT was again a privilege to be asked to deliver the main addresses at the Annual Welsh Conference of the Evangelical Movement of Wales in 2006, and to attempt to expound the true nature of the faith once delivered to the saints. In dedicating this book to the memory of my father, I do so with gratitude. His was the human voice by which I first heard these great truths, and it was under his ministry that, years ago in my early teens, I came to faith in the Lord Jesus Christ.

The Welsh addresses were first published in 2008 under the title *Croes fy Arglwydd*. I am deeply grateful to Dr John Aaron for preparing this translation of the addresses and selecting suitable quotations from English hymns to replace the Welsh originals, and also to Brenda Lewis who edited the final manuscript.

Gwynn Williams
May, 2010

1.

A black picture

*'But now the righteousness of God apart from the law is
revealed, being witnessed by the Law and the Prophets, even
the righteousness of God which is through faith in Jesus Christ
to all and on all who believe. For there is no difference; for all
have sinned and fall short of the glory of God, being justified
freely by his grace through the redemption that is in Christ
Jesus, whom God set forth to be a propitiation by his blood,
through faith, to demonstrate his righteousness, because in his
forbearance God had passed over the sins that were previously
committed, to demonstrate at the present time his
righteousness, that he might be just and the justifier
of the one who has faith in Jesus.'*
(Romans 3:21–26)

At first sight, the paragraph above may seem difficult to
understand, and yet in the judgement of many it is the most
significant paragraph in the whole of the Bible. For here we find
the very heart, the core, of the gospel.

The Christian gospel, of course, is essentially simple. It is a
gospel for *all*, and not everyone has a doctorate! So if this
paragraph describes something simple, why do we have trouble
in understanding it? One answer is that we live in an age when
people are unfamiliar with the vocabulary that is used here; and
when the words seem strange, the concepts become strange too,
and the glorious simplicity of the gospel of Jesus Christ is lost.

Our intention, therefore, is to study Romans 3:21–26, in the
hope that by doing so the simplicity and glory of the gospel will
be evident to us all. There are four reasons for drawing attention
to this particular paragraph.

What is a Christian?

The *first* reason is that it forces us again to consider the question, 'What is a Christian?' As you know, there are many different ideas abroad about this. If you were to ask a number of religious people for a definition, you would find that their answers vary greatly. Some would define Christians as people who follow the example of Jesus Christ: that is, they pursue an appropriate lifestyle and believe that by doing this they are Christians. Others associate being a Christian with going to church or chapel: if you are faithful in maintaining regular attendance on Sundays, they say, you deserve to be called a Christian. Someone else would say, 'Well, if I read the Bible and pray, that surely makes me a Christian.' Others again would argue that entering into some relationship with Jesus is what makes you a Christian. In view of all this, therefore, it will be good for us to remind ourselves of the Bible's definition of a Christian – to go back to the foundations, the biblical description – and then to ask ourselves, 'Do I fit this description?' For surely, if we do not, we have no right to lay claim to the name of Christian.

How does a person become a Christian?

The *second* reason for studying this paragraph is that it will provide us with the answer to another question, namely, 'How does a person become a Christian?' It may be that some young people, when faced with this question, are painfully aware that they are not yet Christians. Or there may be older people who have been interested or even immersed in religion for many years, yet still have profound doubts as to whether they have ever truly arrived, as it were. And so, for them, the nagging question constantly returns: 'What's missing? How may I become a true Christian?' This paragraph of Scripture will answer that question.

It is important, also, for those of us who are Christians to understand the Bible's teaching as to how people become Christians. How we understand this will affect our evangelism. Is our evangelism, and are the methods of our evangelism, compatible with what the Bible teaches on how a person becomes a Christian? Does our evangelism produce true Christians, or those who are Christians in name only? Does it create a type of follower of Jesus, yet one who is not truly saved? It is very necessary, in these uncertain days, for us to ask such questions.

Genuine or counterfeit?

The *third* reason is well illustrated for us by the FBI – the Federal Bureau of Investigation! Let me explain. During the last fifty years or so, the word 'evangelical' has become very popular. It has become an umbrella term encompassing a whole host of people who hold to an enormously wide variety of views on secondary matters. There are differences on methods of worship, differences in attitude towards the baptism of the Holy Spirit, differences as to the gifts of the Spirit, and so on. At one time, all those who came under the umbrella of 'evangelical' were generally agreed as to the essentials of the gospel. But, unfortunately, things have changed. There are now books published by those who claim to be evangelical, and sermons preached by those who call themselves evangelical, whose content is very difficult to reconcile with the teachings of the Scriptures. Some of us, as we read a particular book – one that has come from America, perhaps – or as we listen to a sermon, begin to feel uncomfortable. We may not be able to put our finger on it exactly, but we sense that something does not ring true. The emphasis of the preacher or the tone of the book troubles us; there is some fly in the ointment, we feel, some lack of proper balance in the message, even though we may not discern exactly what is wrong, or know how to deal with it.

How are we to discern what is false? This is where the FBI may help us. They have a department that deals with counterfeit dollars. If you wish to work in that department you must undergo a long course of training that enables you to become expert at recognising counterfeits. You spend the first week of the course studying real dollars; then throughout the second

13

week you study real dollars, and again the third week is spent studying real dollars. For a month, for six months, all you do is study real dollars. And that is the training course! You do not spend time studying the false; all your time is concentrated on the true. And then, just because you have spent so much time with the real, the moment you see the counterfeit you recognise it for what it is. Let us follow the example of the FBI. This passage from Romans takes us to the heart of the true gospel. So let us concentrate on the true, making absolutely sure that we fully understand what is true. If we gain a firm grasp of the truth by doing this, then the counterfeit will be easily recognised.

Our lives as Christians

The *fourth* reason for drawing attention to this paragraph has to do with our personal lives. Many of us feel, perhaps, that our lives as Christians are not very radiant these days. There is not much zeal, not much enthusiasm. And then we find the temptation arising to search out for greater experiences so as to rekindle the thrill. Now, no one denies that there are further experiences to be known in the life of a Christian. There is the experience of Revival – a further dimension, a visitation from God. But as we read the New Testament Epistles we find, in every case, that when Paul arrives at his 'therefore', what he has been doing before the 'therefore' is explaining the truth. The more the Christian sees the wonder of the salvation he already possesses, the greater will be his zeal, sanctification and enthusiasm. There is nothing better than considering the basic truths of the Christian gospel. An understanding of this paragraph should lift us spiritually.

A crucial epistle

The Epistle to the Romans is one of the most important books of the Bible. All the biblical books are important. Each book is inspired; each is infallible; each is authoritative. But when it comes to understanding the biblical message, some books are more significant than others. The first three chapters of Genesis are crucial if you are to understand the rest of the Bible. Chapter 11 of Genesis is also crucial, in that it deals with the key issue of God's covenant with Abraham and with the nation of Israel. And as far as the New Testament is concerned, there is no book more crucial for understanding the whole than the Epistle to the Romans. Commentators have agreed on this throughout the centuries. The book has had immense influence upon the saints through all the Christian ages.

Consider those centuries of darkness in the Middle Ages, when the Roman Catholic Church had lost sight of the heart of the gospel. When Luther pondered the first chapter of this letter, and meditated on verse 17 – 'For in it the righteousness of God is revealed from faith to faith; as it is written, "The just shall live by faith." ' – it was then that the light broke in upon all the Roman Catholic darkness of the previous centuries. As he studied this Epistle, Luther rediscovered that which had been lost. The same thing happened to John Bunyan in the seventeenth century, and in the eighteenth century to John Wesley. It was as they read this letter, and thought over the wonderful truths it contains, that they saw, and were moved, and became a blessing to others. The first eight chapters of Romans form a classic summary of the Christian faith, and this paragraph under consideration is the heart of that faith.

The dark background

When we speak of Christianity we are speaking of 'good news'. That is the literal meaning of the word 'gospel'. It is with this that Paul begins his letter to the Romans: 'Paul, a servant of Jesus Christ, called to be an apostle, separated to the gospel of God' (1:1). And he takes it up again in verse 16, 'I am not ashamed of the gospel of Christ': that is, he is speaking of good news.

But we know from our own experience that very often we do not really appreciate the good until we have contrasted it with what is bad. Have you ever seen Tiger Woods taking on a putt on the eighteenth green – perhaps twenty yards of a putt, or even more? He strikes the ball cleanly and away it goes, straight as a die, and disappears down the hole. 'That looks easy,' you say; 'I'm sure I could do that.' So off you go to the nearby putting green. But, with the hole only four feet away, you find that it takes you four attempts before you succeed! It is only then that you begin to have some appreciation of the level of skill involved.

In the same way, if we wish to understand the good news of the gospel, we must first appreciate what is the bad news. That is exactly what Paul is doing here. He begins by emphasising the bad news. He does not burst out with speaking about Jesus Christ and his good news immediately, for he recognises that we will not appreciate the full glory of the gospel until we have been utterly convinced of the bad news. You cannot discuss salvation without having first understood what it is from which we need to be saved.

Did you ever look in a jeweller's window and see a diamond presented on white paper? No, never. A diamond gleams only when seen against a dark background. Such a stone is set on a black or a deep red backing in order to highlight all its glory. And that is what Paul does here as we begin the Epistle to the Romans. Before beginning to reveal his diamond he spends two and a half chapters painting the background – two and half chapters of background in a book that has only sixteen chapters in all! If the background is not in place, we will not appreciate the main message in all its clarity. And even after those two and a half chapters of background, Paul returns to it yet again in verse 23 of the paragraph under consideration: 'For there is no difference; for all have sinned and fall short of the glory of God.' Although he has already taken great pains to establish this truth, yet on arriving at this key paragraph he has to return to it and remind us once again.

What is that background? 'All have sinned.' It is important to stay a while at this point. A person may make some kind of connection with Jesus Christ for all sorts of reasons, but he cannot know Jesus as a Saviour unless he has some awareness

16

that he himself is lost. Therefore Paul takes his time. 'All have sinned.' All! There are no exceptions. The English Standard Version expresses this very clearly: 'There is no distinction': king or beggar – no distinction; genius or fool – no distinction; man or woman – no distinction; young or old – no distinction. It is with this bad news that the gospel begins.

Perhaps some of you can say, 'Well, I have no problem with that statement at all. I am completely convinced of my sin. I know myself, and I agree with you.' But there may be others who are not fully convinced that they are sinners. Such people might say, 'I accept that I am not perfect, but I am not that bad. I live a reasonably respectable and good life. I don't break the laws of the land. I try to give to charity and so on. I attend church or chapel regularly, and I used to go to Sunday school. There are very many worse people than myself. I've never been drunk or committed adultery. All have sinned? I'm not so sure of that. There is something inside me that rebels against the idea.'

People do not like being called sinners. When I was a minister in Port Talbot, I preached once at a funeral that was attended by an enormous crowd. I was not aware of saying anything dramatic, but the next day one of my church members went to the Post Office in a neighbouring village. As he entered, it became obvious that the postmaster had been at the funeral. He was hardly inside the door when he heard a voice from behind the counter: 'How dare your minister say that I'm a sinner?' The man had been offended. Notice what he said – 'that I'm a sinner!' I did not even know he was in the congregation, and I certainly did not name him or point a finger at him. What I said was, 'All have sinned.' But something had happened. He had appreciated the point, perhaps for the very first time, and he did not like what he had heard.

Indeed, you may not have committed the kind of sins that you read of in the tabloids. But here Paul helps us to understand the nature of the sin to which he is referring. The Authorised Version expresses it in this way: 'For all have sinned and come short of the glory of God.' If you wish to understand this condition, you must bring God into the picture. And not any kind of God! We come before the great and glorious God, the God who is holy and perfect and pure. He is the God of purest light – light so pure that we cannot keep our eyes open before it. Sometimes we find ourselves caught in the dazzling lights of a car and we have to shut our eyes. That is the kind of God that is described in the Bible, a holy and a glorious God. And Paul says, 'That is what I mean when I speak of sin – I am talking of people who have "come short of the glory of God".'

We were created at first in the likeness and image of God. The purpose of our creation was for us to reflect God's glory. But, historically, there was a Fall in the garden of Eden, and we became sinners. Do we now reflect the glory of God, or have we come short of his glory? It is when we begin to think of such things that we begin to realise that we are not as good as we thought, after all. We begin to measure ourselves not against the standard of other people but against the standard of God our Creator. And we 'come short of the glory of God', says Paul.

The Law reveals sin

God knew very well that we would have difficulties with this teaching, and so, right from the beginning of his Bible, he provided a way to help us appreciate it. Notice the words that come just before the paragraph we are considering: 'by the law is the knowledge of sin'. God wishes us to see this truth; he wishes sinners to understand that they are sinners. He therefore gave us the Law, so that man, by measuring himself against that Law, will understand that he is a sinner. That Law is to be found in the Old Testament, in the five books of Moses and, in particular, in the Ten Commandments.

If we had time, we could go through all the commandments, showing how each of them in turn promotes in us a consciousness of sin. Let me give one example from the first part of the Law. Think of that commandment that has to do with other gods. May I ask you a question – and ask you to answer it immediately, without weighing it up too much? It is this: What is the most important thing in your life?

Was your immediate answer, 'God'? To fail to answer it immediately in this way is ungodliness: 'You shall have no other gods before me.' God demands the uppermost place in men's hearts, and if anything else takes that foremost place it means that God has been pushed to the side. That is ungodliness. Some people will say, 'But there is still a little place for God in my heart, even though he is to the side.' But that is to make God a hobby, and he demands to be at the centre: 'And you shall love the Lord your God', said Jesus Christ, 'with all your heart, with all your soul, with all your mind, and with all your strength' (Mark 12:30). The Law teaches us of sin, and it makes us aware of sin. There may be many other things that are central in our lives, things that in themselves are perfectly legitimate and acceptable. But God is not happy with that situation. He demands the central position, and to refuse to give him that which is his right is to be ungodly.

Or we could take a commandment from the second part of the Law: 'Do not kill.' Perhaps we breathe a slight sigh of relief here: 'Well, at least I've never killed anybody.' But let us turn to the New Testament and read the words of Jesus Christ: 'But I say to you that whoever is angry with his brother without a cause shall be in danger of the judgement. And whoever says to his brother, "Raca!" [that is, "Empty head!"] shall be in danger of the council. But whoever says, "You fool!" shall be in danger of hell fire' (Matthew 5:22). Your situation is a little less comfortable now, is it not? You have lost your temper. You have become angry with your brother, and perhaps at some point you may even have said, 'I could have killed him.' The Law emphasises to us our sin, because there is something inside us that wishes to close our eyes to the fact. But God would have us see it, and he provides help for us so that we may see it. 'All have sinned.'

Jesus Christ sums up the matter in Mark 7:21–23. Notice the mix of sins that he points out, both tabloid sins and heart sins: 'For from within, out of the heart of men, proceed evil thoughts, adulteries, fornications, murders, thefts, covetousness, wickedness, deceit, licentiousness, an evil eye, blasphemy, pride, foolishness. All these evil things come from within and defile a man.' That is our state – all have sinned.

For two and a half chapters Paul has been establishing this truth. He deals first, in the opening chapter, with the Gentiles. These are people without God, whom God has given up because they had rejected him, and the consequence of this is the immorality that follows. Then, in the second chapter, he deals with the Jews, a religious people, those who thought that they were keeping the Law. He proceeds to undermine all their self-confidence and self-righteousness, until they also are placed in such a corner that they have to acknowledge that they too are sinners.

Do we now see, then, that this is where we must start? There is no point in continuing with the rest of the paragraph – no point whatsoever – unless we see this: 'All have sinned and fall short of the glory of God.'

What does it matter?

But we are living in the twenty-first century, and the man in the street asks, 'But what does it matter? All right, we're sinners! Great! We'll just carry on. We'll sin. After all, we're only here for a few years. We'll do whatever seems right in our own eyes. Why do we have to bother about sin? Why worry about whether or not we reflect the glory of God?' That is the way people speak today, isn't it?

Yet he would be a very foolish man to speak like that. You could take him aside and say, 'Wait a minute. Don't you understand what sin does, how much suffering it causes to many people? Shouldn't you do something about sin because of its negative results? And don't you sometimes in your own heart, for example, have pangs of conscience?'

Do we know something of this? The hymn-writer describes it as 'Conscience roaring in my breast.' We have done something we know very well we should not have done; we feel a measure of guilt or embarrassment about it, and we hope no one finds out about it. We have private thoughts that torment us, and perhaps in our concern over them we are unable to sleep at night. Conscience is pricking. Perhaps you lost your temper with someone during the day – maybe with a friend of yours. You said something very unwise and unkind, and you cannot understand what came over you. Your conscience continually troubles you. It is a miserable and upsetting time. Would not life be better if there were no sin there in the first place – a life of peace without all the roaring of conscience, the experience of peace of heart with no uneasiness to trouble us?

But sin not only causes us problems personally; it is also the cause of friction between people. Are there not continuous quarrels in this world because of sin? Think of Christmas Day. This is surely a time for everyone to be happy, and yet for some reason the children choose to be disobedient. They have to be spoken to, and the whole day is spoilt because of disobedience. Or think of the workplace. Something is said that leads to unkind words or unfair criticism, and as a result the place is full of tension and stress. Or, within a marriage, lust raises its head, adultery results, and the crash that follows brings heartbreak to all concerned and misery for the children. Would not the world be a happier place without sin?

Again, think of the problems that arise between nations: ambition, pride and the longing for lands and wealth prevail, and there are wars and rumours of wars. Are not the results of sin in society a reason for seeking a solution to the problem? Should we not try to deal with sin because of its influence on us and on others?

The wrath of God
What has Paul to say about these things? The wonder is that he says nothing of them. Not a word! We have to deal with the problem of sin, says Paul, not because it upsets us or other people. It is much worse than that; the situation is truly black. Here is his statement on the sinfulness of man: 'The wrath of God is revealed from heaven against all ungodliness and

unrighteousness of men' (Romans 1:18). What a terrifying statement of the situation! The heart of the problem is that God is being offended, that God's wrath is opposed to sinners. That is the great issue. Sin is not just something that causes personal guilt, or friction in society, or that drives nations to war, but sin is something that brings all of mankind under the wrath of God. There is, of course, very little mention of the wrath of God today. That is not the way to maintain a congregation, people say: 'Don't preach on wrath, or they will all leave.' But when we consider that Paul, at the beginning of his explanation of Christianity, spends no less than two and a half chapters drawing attention to the fact that we are all sinners under God's wrath, such a view presents difficulties. Do we know better that the inspired apostle?

God's Word states, 'The wrath of God is revealed...' But where is it revealed? Well, there are a number of accounts in the Old Testament where we see the wrath of God being revealed in specific historical events. And in the New Testament it is revealed by the words of the Lord Jesus Christ himself. In his parables, for example, every reference to heaven is contrasted to a reference to hell. And in his teaching, without mincing matters, he who has a perfect knowledge of his Father speaks constantly and resolutely of the wrath of God.

What is this wrath? Does God lose his temper with us? No, he does not. The wrath of God is a constant state of mind, not a passing, arbitrary feeling. It is the irrevocable opposition of the Holy to anything that is not holy. It is the rejection of everything that does not conform to his will. The Old Testament speaks of God as one who is 'of purer eyes than to behold evil' (Habakkuk 1:13). Sin is odious in his sight and abhorrent to him. He has to turn away from it; it is so contrary to his absolute purity.

Again, Jesus Christ does not mince matters when he speaks of hell. He describes it as a place of weeping and of gnashing of teeth. He speaks of outer darkness and of inextinguishable flame. This is Jesus Christ speaking! Do not attempt to differentiate between the teaching of Paul and the teaching of Jesus; there is no difference. Do not attempt to drive a wedge between the Old Testament and the words of Jesus Christ; it is the same teaching. For Jesus Christ is holy; he himself is a divine person, and so the rejection of sin which is inherent in the Father is inherent in him also. They are one God. And when Jesus Christ speaks of hell, he knows what it is he is describing. There is the blackness and the darkness; that is the background.

Paul closes his discussion of the state of mankind with the horrifying words, 'that…all the world may become guilty before God' (Romans 3:19). It is as if he is saying, 'There is no point at all in your reading my letter further if you have not understood my argument up to this point. The whole world is guilty before God.' This is true for every one of us. Have you arrived at this point yet?

'Every mouth…stopped'

Let us consider a court of law. Imagine that a court is in session and the accused is in the dock. The prosecutor presents the evidence against him, and afterwards the lawyer representing the accused will do his best for him. I remember Perry Mason on television acting as a lawyer for the defence. He had a particular style. A prosecutor might disclose some fact, and he would immediately stand up and shout, 'Objection!' Later on, when some further fact of evidence was revealed, the shout of 'Objection!' would ring through the court once again.

Imagine a court where the prosecutor has a mass of evidence to present against a defendant. At the beginning, the defence frequently calls 'Objection!', but as the day proceeds and the evidence becomes more and more compelling, those calls gradually die away. The defence cannot think of anything to say. And then, when a huge incriminating mass of evidence against the defendant has been disclosed, the judge asks, 'Have you anything to say?' The defence is silent – their mouths have been shut. It is evident to everyone in court that the defendant is guilty – evident both to jury and judge. All that remains is to pass a formal verdict of guilt and to sentence the criminal. And so Paul states, 'We know that whatever the law says, it says to those who are under the law, that every mouth may be stopped ...' (verse 19). It is at this point, and nowhere else, that the Christian life begins – when our mouths have been stopped in the presence of the holy God.

Have you arrived at this point yet? What Paul is doing here is explaining how people enter the Christian life. He is explaining what Christianity is, what the gospel is. He takes his time to do this. He has been inspired to do so by God himself, and woe betide us if we fail to pay attention to what he says! Have we realised our sinfulness? Have we been convicted of our guilt? Have we seen the wrath of God as something real that is opposed to us, and have our mouths been stopped?

Sometimes we see Jesus Christ stopping people's mouths. Do you remember the rich young man that came to him to ask him a question about eternal life? He received a reply, but he went away saddened, and with his mouth stopped. That man had to see that he was a sinner. And that is where true conversion begins, when a man realises that he must be right before God, that he is not right before God, and that there is nothing he can do about it. Lost! Under the wrath of God! Helpless!

We do not begin with Jesus Christ. We begin by standing before God with our mouths stopped – 'without one plea,' says the hymnist – knowing that we are guilty and deserve the frown of heaven.

2.

Hope of salvation

*'But now the righteousness of God...is revealed, being
witnessed by the Law and the Prophets, even the
righteousness of God which is through faith in Jesus Christ...
being justified freely by his grace...'*
(Romans 3:21, 22, 24)

Before building a house, foundations must be carefully laid. As
we have seen, at the beginning of his letter to the Romans, Paul
has taken great pains to establish the foundation. We – all of us,
whether pagan or religious – have come short of the glory of
God: 'For there is no difference; for all have sinned and fall short
of the glory of God' (Romans 3:22, 23). The consequence is that
we are all under God's wrath – that is the natural state of each
one of us: 'The wrath of God is revealed from heaven against all
ungodliness and unrighteousness of men' (Romans 1:18).

That is where the Christian life begins. It begins with an
awareness of this abysmal condition and state, an appreciation of
the fact that we are under the judgement of God, and that his
holy Law puts a stop to every mouth. Indeed, it is Christ's own
testimony that the initial work of the Holy Spirit in any
individual is the conviction of sin, of righteousness, and of
judgement (John 16:8). The old Welsh saints used to say that
every Christian life began at *'bwlch yr argyhoeddiad'* ('the
pass of conviction').

The nature of conversion
At this point we must deal with a particular problem that may
arise. Some will say, 'Hold on a minute! Does everyone who
comes to know Jesus Christ have to pass through an experience
of conviction? Don't the Gospels describe some who enter into a

relationship with Christ without ever mentioning any awareness of sin? There are experiences in the Gospels that seem to be different from the teachings of the Epistles.'

But this cannot be so, for the Scriptures are one. We must therefore consider events recorded in the life of Jesus Christ and ask ourselves what is happening here. The point is this: while it is true that many different kinds of people come to Jesus Christ in the Gospels and enter into some kind of relationship with him, they do not all experience that relationship that ensures salvation. Think, for example, of the ten lepers mentioned in Luke 17. They were suffering from a physical disease, and they approached Jesus Christ. He sent them to the priest, and on their way all of them were healed. Their physical problems were solved, certainly, but were they all saved, and will they all be in heaven? The account suggests strongly that they will not, because only one of them returned to thank Jesus and to give glory to God. Christ commends that individual for his faith. What of the other nine? To use contemporary language, their 'felt needs' were satisfied, but are they among the saved? We cannot be sure – the Bible does not provide an answer one way or the other.

But when we consider the feeding of the five thousand, the situation is perfectly clear. Were all five thousand who were fed by the loaves saved through that experience? Clearly they were not. The next day, when they were still following him, Christ stated: '…you seek me, not because you saw the signs [that is, the clear pointers that Christ is the Son of God], but because you ate of the loaves and were filled' (John 6:26). That was the level of their relationship with Christ. Their experience of him rose no higher than 'What good can we get out of it?' So they were evidently not converted.

The case of the paralytic man is very different. Christ tells him, 'Son, your sins are forgiven' (Mark 2:5), so there is a clear difference here. Then consider the case of Judas Iscariot. Despite a relatively close relationship with Jesus for three years, it was not a saving relationship. He remained a 'son of perdition', a lost soul (John 17:12).

These few examples are sufficient to demonstrate that we cannot prove the true nature of conversion simply from events described in the Gospels. The three-year period of Christ's public ministry was unique. When physically present on earth, Jesus Christ naturally came into contact with hundreds of people in all kinds of different ways. While each of these people featured in the narrative of Christ's life, we cannot on that basis form a general doctrine of conversion, or formulate principles. These accounts are descriptive, not prescriptive. Because of this, any evangelising based on the Gospels must be approached very carefully.

Have the Gospels, then, nothing to say to us of the way of salvation? Yes, of course they have, but not so much from the events of Jesus Christ's life as from his teaching.

At this point another problem often arises: Isn't the teaching of Jesus Christ very different from the teaching of Paul? This question must be answered head on with a resounding no! We do not have the space to look at all Christ's teaching, but let us consider the Sermon on the Mount for a moment (Matthew 5–7). This is a key element in his teaching, and it begins with the words, 'Blessed are the poor in spirit.' Who are these but souls under conviction – knowing they are sinners and keenly aware of the poverty of their souls? Then, 'Blessed are those who mourn' (as a consequence of this conviction); and again, 'Blessed are those who hunger and thirst for righteousness.' With these words we find ourselves right in the middle of chapter 3 of Paul's Epistle to the Romans. Christ begins his Sermon on the Mount by speaking of mourning for sin and the need of righteousness. And in case any have not appreciated his emphasis, he closes his sermon by exhorting, 'Enter by the narrow gate; for wide is the gate and broad is the way that leads to destruction, and there are many who go in by it. Because narrow is the gate and difficult is the way which leads to life, and there are few who find it' (7:13–14). There is no difference on this point between the Gospels and the Epistles. Both speak of conversion in terms of awareness of sin, the experience of the narrow gate, and the 'pass' of conviction.

The genius of John Bunyan is seen in the way he portrays all these elements in his *Pilgrim's Progress*. The pilgrim has become aware of sin, and then comes the moment when he passes through the wicket-gate. Having passed through, laden with his burden (the conviction of sin), he soon arrives at the cross, and there his burden falls away. But here is an interesting point: as he proceeds, walking between two high walls, two characters suddenly jump over the wall and begin to accompany him. Pilgrim argues with them: 'Listen, you must not do this. You should have come in through the gate that stands at the beginning of the way.' They answered that it was the tradition of their countrymen to make a short cut of it and jump over the wall. And we need to ask ourselves, 'Have we jumped over the wall?' It is possible for us to maintain a relationship with Jesus Christ that does not in any way lead to salvation.

There are some who view Jesus Christ only as a good example, and they claim a relationship with him because they seek to follow his example. Others maintain a formal relationship with him by attending church and so on. It is interesting to note the names of those who jumped over the wall in *Pilgrim's Progress*: one was called Formalist and the other Hypocrisy. It is possible for you to be surrounded by religion and religious matters, and yet not to have entered by the right way – you have jumped over the wall. And because you did not enter by the gate of conviction, and you never felt the burden on your back and were never at the foot of the cross, you will not arrive at the end of the journey, the Celestial City. There are many kinds of relationship with Jesus Christ, but not all of them will save you. The Bible explains carefully the way that does save.

The consequences for evangelism

These truths will certainly affect the way we evangelise. If we believe that the process of conversion begins with the conviction of sin, it becomes essential for us, when we preach, to wield those weapons which convince of sin – that is, to proclaim the

Law, the sinfulness of man, and the wrath of God. If that is the Bible's way of saving people, then we are bound to operate in accord with the biblical testimony.

This means that there is no place for frivolity in evangelism. It is a matter of supreme seriousness; we are addressing those who are under wrath. We are attempting to rescue them from that wrath by presenting to them the good tidings of great joy. It is a matter of an eternity in heaven or an eternity in hell. And if the first step is to become aware of sin and of death, then we must take care that the schoolmaster that God himself has appointed to bring people to that awareness, namely the Law, has its appropriate place in our sermons. 'The law was our tutor to bring us to Christ' (Galatians 3:24). That is the way God works.

Of course, we are people of our own day and age. And that is part of the problem. Our age has its ways of influencing people, persuading them to change their minds and getting them to take up various causes. One such method is the advertising that assails our eyes, the direct psychological and emotional persuasion that has such an effect upon us. It becomes all too easy for us, therefore, to conclude that we must also evangelise by this method. But the Scripture states that 'faith comes by hearing' (Romans 10:17), not by the eye. Why? What you hear goes immediately to the mind, not to the feelings or emotions. 'Come now,' says God, 'and let us reason together' (Isaiah 1:18). This does not mean that we are not to use pictures and illustrations to strengthen our reasoning, but it is the reasoning that is to have priority, the appeal to the mind, not the immediate assault upon the feelings.

In a word, we must allow the Bible to control the content of the message and the method of proclaiming that message to those who are under the wrath of God. Not to do this is tantamount to encouraging them to jump over the wall. And they will not thank us for that in eternity.

A basic question

Having said all this, we arrive at a basic question: *How can we*

29

be right before God? The Bible's answer, as we see in this paragraph (Romans 3:21–26), is that we enter into a right relationship with God by being justified by faith. It is a well-known fact that, for a long period in the history of the Church, people lost sight of this glorious and central truth with respect to becoming a Christian. Then, in the sixteenth century, it was rediscovered in a remarkable way by Martin Luther, under the guidance of the Holy Spirit.

But before proceeding with an explanation of justification by faith, we must emphasise that there is nothing more important for us to understand than this. For if we do not appreciate the teaching of this section of Scripture, the whole of our Christianity is sure to be skewed from this point onwards. It brings us to the heart of the matter, and if we are not correct at the heart, everything else will be misdirected.

Let us consider the passage, therefore, phrase by phrase. We have been picturing man in his lostness, in sin and under the wrath of God. He has not a glimmer of hope from anywhere. And we then come to the words at the beginning of verse 21, 'But now'. Paul is clearly referring to some historical event that has only recently occurred: 'But now, in our own age, something has happened.' And we understand, of course, that he is referring to the coming of the Lord Jesus Christ into the world. He is referring to his miraculous birth at Bethlehem, his perfect life on earth, his death upon the cross, his resurrection, and then his ascension forty days later. Something has happened, he declares – an event that has changed that picture of complete hopelessness. We have seen that God, through his Law, has stopped every mouth, that 'all the world may become guilty before God'. The next step is for us to be able to say, 'But now!' Are you, in the midst of the hopelessness, able to say, 'But now!'?

A word in passing to believers: As we know, the devil is able to approach us and attack us, bringing his accusations. We often fall into sin, and the evil one will say, 'Look at you. You're a sorry kind of Christian. How can you imagine that you are saved? Look at the state of your life.' What do you do at such times? Do you say to the devil, 'But now!'? When all the problems of life gather about your head and you feel that you are sinking, can you in the midst of it all say, 'But now!'? That is conversion – for a man to be able to say, 'But now!' And Paul is about to explain the significance of these words – the wonderful fact that transforms the situation and brings a glorious hope to sinners.

'The righteousness of God'
'What happens? God does something. 'But now the righteousness of God...is revealed' (Romans 3:21). It is interesting to note that although he is speaking of the coming of the Lord Jesus, he does not name Christ at all. What he sees to be happening is the revealing of the righteousness of God. It is to God that he first gives his attention. The same emphasis is seen in the opening verse of the Epistle: 'Paul, a servant of Jesus Christ, called to be an apostle, separated to the gospel of God'. We might expect, 'called to the gospel of Jesus Christ'. But it is God's gospel first. As he begins his explanation of 'But now', it is God who has his attention; it is God who has acted.

Now we know that some Christians – and we do not doubt for a moment the sincerity of their faith or their zeal – hardly speak at all of God the Father. They speak of Jesus continually and address him constantly in their prayers, but there is hardly any mention of the Father. One well-known preacher – who preached a long series on Romans – said that this was a most serious matter. Why? For this reason: the purpose of the gospel is not to bring us to Jesus Christ but to bring us to God. The great tragedy of our situation is that we are under the wrath of God, and the purpose of the gospel is to bring us to peace with God. This is not in any way to belittle Jesus Christ, as we shall see later, but it is the Father who must have first place in our thoughts. In some circles today there is a danger of distancing the Father and moving him to one side.

Jesus Christ himself taught us to pray, 'Our Father'. Christ

31

knew that the chief purpose of all his work and ministry was to bring us to the Father. And as we search the Scriptures, we understand that it is the Father who has sent forth this wonderful gospel. Consider the most famous verse in the New Testament: 'For God so loved the world that he gave his only begotten Son' (John 3:16). Who is it that is pictured here? It is the Father. The source of salvation is the love of the Father. The Father views his creatures, made in his own image and likeness, and sees them ruined by the Fall and in utter hopelessness. And in his grace and mercy he determines to act. And so Paul declares, 'But now the righteousness of God…is revealed'. God the Father moves to save sinners. How disastrous it would be to push the Father to one side!

'The Law and the Prophets'
To return to our subject, it is God's righteousness that has been revealed. The action is God's; but it was no unexpected action. It was not done in haste, as if God, in a panic, hurriedly sent his Son into the world to fulfil the work of salvation. No, '…being witnessed by the Law and the Prophets' (verse 21). This is one of the simplest phrases of the paragraph. It tells us that there was no surprise in the sending of Jesus Christ into the world to be a Saviour. The whole of the Law (that is, the five books of Moses) and the prophets had foretold all that would occur. We may go right back to Genesis to find the promise, 'I will put enmity between you and the woman, and between your seed and her Seed; he shall bruise your head, and you shall bruise his heel' (Genesis 3:15). Christ is there, in the Old Testament. We are familiar with chapters 9 and 11 of Isaiah – those portions read at Christmas-time about the Son, born of a virgin, the mighty God, the everlasting Father; and we are also familiar with all that is contained in Isaiah 53. The Law and the prophets speak of the day of the revelation of the righteousness of God.

The First Epistle of Peter sums up the matter: 'Of this salvation the prophets have inquired and searched diligently, who prophesied of the grace that would come to you…' (1 Peter

1:10–12). This was a vital element of the mission of the prophets – preparing the way, and foretelling the wonderful actions taken by God to save sinners that lay under his wrath.

Some people disregard the Old Testament. Only the New Testament deserves our attention, they say; the Old Testament is old-fashioned. But if the Old Testament and the Law are our schoolmaster or tutor to teach us an awareness of sin and to bring us eventually to Christ (Galatians 3:24), then we stand in need of the Law in order to know conviction. Furthermore, the apostle tells us that the Old Testament is our schoolmaster in another sense: it is our teacher, for it tells us of the One who is to come. The Law and the prophets testify to this remarkable event in the history of mankind. All point to the coming of the Lord Jesus Christ, at that critical moment when the wonderful plan of salvation was fully acted out and accomplished on the stage of world history.

It is interesting to note what Paul says. He is speaking of the coming of Christ, but what he sees in his mind's eye is the revelation of the glory of God. He does not say that he sees a revelation of the forgiveness of sins. There is much more to justification than the forgiveness of sins. Paul chooses his words, under the influence of the Holy Spirit, with deliberate and solemn care. That which is revealed from heaven is 'the righteousness of God'. This is the gospel. Jesus Christ tells a parable of someone attending a wedding feast, but although he had replied to the invitation he was thrown out because he did not have the correct dress. There is more to going to heaven than having my sins forgiven. Being 'clothed in righteousness divine' belongs to it too.

The meaning of justification

We must now ask what is meant by receiving this righteousness, by being 'justified'. What happens to a sinner when he or she is justified? Clearly, according to Paul, it is something wonderful and glorious.

Let us visit the court of law again. Here, for the accused in the dock, there is only one of two outcomes: he will either be found guilty, the evidence against him being unanswerable, or he will be found not guilty. Those are the two possibilities. If he is guilty, we say he is condemned, and because he is condemned he will receive punishment. What does justification mean? It is the opposite of condemnation. When the judge, on the basis of the evidence, finds the accused not guilty, he justifies him. His arguments have been accepted, and because he is justified he may go free; there is no need for him to bear any punishment or fulfil any penance.

There is a day coming when we shall all have to stand before God at the judgement court of heaven, and there every mouth will be stopped. A moment will come when the great Judge, the eternal God, will pronounce his sentence. The evidence against us is clear and undeniable. We shall have no argument; we are all guilty, and the Judge has made his judgement. And here we have the crux of the good news of the Bible: on the Last Day, this great and holy God will pronounce an innumerable company of people *not guilty*. The ungodly will be justified! A sinner who deserves punishment will be declared innocent. He deserves the frown of heaven, but he receives a pronouncement of peace and reconciliation. The gospel is God's plan for justifying the ungodly – God declaring the guilty to be innocent!

An enormous problem

But now a problem arises. Imagine such circumstances arising in a court in our country. The judge takes his seat, and before him is brought one whom everyone knows to be guilty. Yet, to the amazement of all, the judge pronounces him 'Not guilty'. Imagine the headlines in the next day's tabloids! Then suppose that, the following day, he does exactly the same for some other villain. The papers would cry out that the judge had lost his senses; he must have become unbalanced, to be freeing those who are clearly criminal! Others might accuse him of accepting bribes, or allege some other form of corruption. As he continued with such decisions day after day we can well imagine what a storm would be raised in the land. Instead of administering justice, this judge is releasing transgressors and proclaiming lawbreakers to be innocent!

But that is exactly what God does. And the questions shout out at us. Why is God acting in this way? How on earth is he able to do it? It is good tidings of great joy, certainly, to those who are being released, but why is it happening? It seems to make no sense that this God of laws and commandments, this God whose wrath is against us, is apparently changing his mind completely and redeeming a throng of people. How can this be?

Grace

At this point we arrive at Christianity's greatest word: 'being justified freely by his grace', says Paul (verse 24). Here is the answer – grace. The love, mercy and grace of God are poured out on undeserving sinners. C. S. Lewis was once asked the question, 'What is the difference between Christianity and all the other religions of the world?' He answered with one word: 'Grace'. The gospel is a gospel of grace. This is what we find in Ephesians, chapter 2: 'For by grace you have been saved through faith, and that not of yourselves; it is the gift of God' (Ephesians 2:8).

Notice the word 'freely'. Deep within ourselves we have that sense of wishing to be able to pay for everything; but this amazing blessing is free! Here is good news for every one of us. Grace works impartially. We might imagine a human judge releasing certain individuals because of a family relationship, or because they are members of the same Masonic lodge. But God acts completely from grace, and freely.

There is hope for everyone here. If a price had to be paid, the rich would have an advantage. But grace is good news even for the poorest person without a penny in his pocket. If salvation depended on a doctrinal understanding of the Scriptures, then those with higher intellectual abilities would be at an advantage. But no, we are justified by God's grace, freely. Perhaps some sinner might feel that he is not good enough to be among the host of the redeemed. The good news is that that is no barrier. All have sinned and fall short of the glory of God, but all may also hope to be part of that innumerable crowd on the Last Day. Are you, therefore, one of them? We shall consider later who they are that make up that innumerable throng, but the possibility of being among them is yours presently. That hope is held up before you, that God on the Last Day will declare over you, 'Not guilty'.

Think for a moment of the earthly court of law, and of the poor, trembling defendant in the dock expecting the worst. And then the judgement is heard: 'Not guilty'. You can imagine his head lifting, his face lighting up. 'Wonderful!' He jumps out of the dock, perhaps, and bounds down the street. 'I'm free! I've been found not guilty.' What is the source of our streams of joy as believers? They begin here, with the awareness of God's grace forgiving and justifying sinners, and that freely.

Who is a pardoning God like Thee?
Or who has grace so rich and free?

Samuel Davies (1723–61)

Yet, though we read of God's grace forgiving freely, the problem remains. The question is still unanswered: 'Only a corrupt judge could pronounce the guilty to be not guilty. How can God be just, and also justify the ungodly?' In the remainder of this wonderful passage (verses 24–26), we are given a complete answer.

3.

'Atonement now is made'

'...being justified freely by his grace through the redemption
that is in Christ Jesus, whom God set forth to be a
propitiation...to demonstrate his righteousness, because
in his forbearance God had passed over the sins that
were previously committed'
(Romans 3: 24–25)

In Pilgrim's Progress, soon after the pilgrim has been convicted
of sin, he arrives at the foot of the cross. When we draw near to
the cross, we are approaching a mystery, something the human
mind can never fully comprehend. There are other similar
mysteries in the Christian faith. The teaching concerning the
Trinity, for example, is a mystery: Three in One, and One in
Three! For all the explanations, discussions and books on the
theme, ultimately we do not understand it. Or take the Person
of the Lord Jesus Christ, described by the Welsh hymn-writer
Ann Griffiths as

Two natures in One Person,
Inseparably joined.

The same is true of the cross. What is the relationship between
the death of Christ on Calvary's cross, two thousand years ago,
and the fact that we may be justified by faith? According to
Charles Wesley,

'Tis mystery all! The Immortal dies!
Who can explore His strange design?

And another Welsh hymn-writer, William Williams, Pantycelyn,
wrote:

37

Eternity, though infinite,
Is short enough to trace
The virtues of His healing wounds,
The wonders of His grace.

We have already considered the amazing activity of God in pronouncing an innumerable number of guilty, undeserving persons innocent, and we have noted the problem. Is not God, by justifying the ungodly, compromising his own character? Is he not, by such deeds, acting contrary to his own just and righteous nature? We considered the case of a judge in a British court, and saw how, if he were to act in this manner, it would cause an immediate reaction in society and provoke protest against releasing the guilty without punishment. We must therefore face the question: how can God justify the ungodly and yet remain just himself?

I was a student at Aberystwyth during the sixties of the last century. It was a decade full of continual protest by *Cymdeithas yr Iaith Gymraeg* (The Welsh Language Society). They pulled down English-language road signs, carried them to the nearest police station and left them in a pile on the ground. These students had to be taken to court and charged. They were not thieves, for they had returned the signs to the authorities, so other charges were brought against them: damage to property, public nuisance, and so on. It was expected that they would each be fined, but as poor students they had little money, if any, to pay such fines. The authorities, for their part, were reluctant to fill the prisons with students (and that for fairly trivial crimes), for they would then be taking up places required for real criminals. So the situation presented all kinds of problems. In the event, some supporters of *Cymdeithas yr Iaith* belonging to the middle classes attended the court hearings, and as the fines were imposed, these people would take out their chequebooks and pay them. With this everyone was content: the prison governors were glad not to have to fill their prisons with students; the law of the land was satisfied in that its demands were met, and the judges were more than happy to be rid of these troublesome cases by receiving the cheques and releasing the students. They were completely within their rights to do this, as the price had been paid. The law's demands had been satisfied, and the transgressors were free.

This is exactly what Paul is arguing here: '...being justified freely by his grace through the redemption that is in Christ Jesus, whom God set forth to be a propitiation' (verses 24–25). We see, therefore, that the justification of the ungodly is an action that is necessarily and inseparably associated with the death of the Lord Jesus Christ. Jesus Christ came into the world in order not only to *proclaim* salvation, but also to *accomplish* that salvation: 'For the Son of Man has come to seek and to save that which was lost' (Luke 19:10).

Paul uses two words in this passage that particularly help us to understand his meaning. They are words that convey images or pictures from everyday life. That is the way God takes to lead us into the mysteries of his character and work. Instead of speaking in abstract, absolute terms – terms that we would fail to comprehend – he gives us pictures and illustrations. And as we study these illustrations, even though we shall certainly not grasp the whole, we may be brought to understand all that is presently necessary for us to know.

Redemption

The first word is *redemption*. God justifies 'through the redemption that is in Christ Jesus'. This word takes us immediately into the world of commerce, of buying and selling – and, in Roman times particularly, the world of buying and selling slaves. Slave-markets were very common, and in these markets it was also possible for a slave to buy his liberty. He could either pay the required price (the ransom) himself, or another might do this for him.

As Jesus Christ thought of the death that lay before him, he used the picture of slavery: 'For even the Son of Man did not come to be served, but to serve, and to give his life a ransom for

39

many' (Mark 10:45). Christ was saying that he had come to do the work of salvation, and that this involved paying a price. We are all enslaved in our sin and wickedness, for, as we have seen, 'All have sinned and fall short of the glory of God', and there is no escape from this condition without the paying of a price. And the price, or ransom, is the life of the Lord Jesus.

Atonement

The second word is *atonement*. The word 'propitiation' is used in most English versions of the Bible, but I will make use of the translation found in this verse in William Morgan's Welsh Bible (and also in the New International Version).

We must spend time over this word for two reasons. First, the idea of atonement or propitiation has been viewed with scorn by many in the past; and still today the suggestion that Christ's death is to be understood in terms of an atonement is being mocked and ridiculed. Secondly, we shall never appreciate the nature and depths of the suffering of Christ until we get to grips with the concept of atonement. Only to the degree that we understand the atonement of the cross will we be able to echo the words of Isaac Watts:

> *Thus might I hide my blushing face,*
> *While his dear cross appears;*
> *Dissolve my heart in thankfulness,*
> *And melt my eyes to tears.*

It is only by seeing something of the infinite depths of the atonement that we shall be moved in the depths of our own hearts and begin to appreciate what the Son accomplished when he died on the cross.

The meaning of 'atonement'

What does the word 'atonement' mean? If we consult a dictionary we find that 'to atone' means to reconcile or pacify. A problem may have arisen between two people, for example. One of them has been offended by the other and needs to be reconciled. How can that be done? Once again, the best way of explaining is by illustration. Living as we do in a litigious society, where compensation is claimed for nearly everything, we can look at it in terms of the paying of compensation or damages.

Imagine a car accident. A driver under the influence of alcohol cannot control his car, and an accident occurs. He is not much hurt himself, but the driver of the second car is very seriously injured, his car is a write-off and he is unable to work for a long time. The case is brought to court; the drunk driver is found guilty, and the second driver claims damages. The judge now has to decide how much the guilty person should pay for sufficient reparation to be made, and he appoints a sum. Notice the four elements in this simple illustration: the offence – namely, the accident; the transgressor or offender – the drunken driver; the person who has been offended; and the price, or compensation, that must be paid. This is exactly what we find in the Scriptures. Let us consider these four elements as they arise in our relationship with God.

What is the offence? 'All have sinned and fall short of the glory of God.' This is the transgression: sin and rebellion against God. Another word used for this is 'ungodliness'. Man rejects God; he does not wish God to be part of his life. Perhaps he denies the very existence of God. He blasphemes his name, ignores him, and makes his own idols. And inseparable from this ungodliness is unrighteousness: that is, his sins against his fellow creatures.

Who is the offender? 'All have sinned.' We are all in the same boat here. We saw that Paul took two and a half chapters to prove that both Jews and Gentiles are transgressors. He brought his argument to the point where 'every mouth [is] stopped'. In the judgement of God everybody is guilty. We are all, without exception, offenders.

Who has been offended? In the illustration given this was perfectly clear: it is the person who was so seriously injured and lost money because he could not work. He was angry with the one who caused the accident, and compensation was needed to appease that anger. So it is with God. The main problem with sin, as we have seen, is that 'the wrath of God is revealed from heaven against all ungodliness and unrighteousness of men' (Romans 1:18). This does not mean that God loses his temper. It rather describes that constant and resolute rejection by God of anything that is contrary to his nature and will.

What is the atonement? In the illustration, it is the cheque that is paid, making reparation to the one who is offended. What is the atonement of the Scriptures? It is Jesus Christ. He is the one who satisfies the wrath of the Father.

Opposition to the doctrine

Many people attack this doctrine. An objector might argue, 'Ugh! How is this different from sheer paganism? Isn't this what pagans believe – that they can influence the gods and change their minds by sacrificing to them?'

There are many different illustrations that offer themselves at this point, but let us turn to Greek mythology. Do you remember the story of Helen of Troy? She so captured the heart of Paris of Troy that he raided the Greeks and carried her away. The Greek king, Agamemnon, raised an army to right the wrong done to his brother, Helen's husband. They embark on their ships to set sail for Troy, but the winds are against them and they cannot move. They need, therefore, to sacrifice to the gods, to get them to change their minds. Agamemnon sends for his daughter and sacrifices her to the gods to appease them. And, indeed, it works! The death of the girl seems to satisfy the gods and dissipate their anger. The winds change, and Agamemnon and his men sail for Troy.

A pagan idea?

'And isn't that your doctrine?' they say. 'What's the difference between your idea of atonement and what we find in that mythology? A sacrifice changing the mind of God! A sacrifice appeasing his wrath and pacifying him! That's a pagan idea, and that's exactly your view of the atonement.'

We answer with certainty, 'No, not at all!' One extraordinarily important fact has been omitted, and with this all-significant fact we rise from the pagan world to the glorious world of Christian salvation. For the fact that transforms the situation is this: it is God himself, and not man, who provided the sacrifice.

Look at it in verses 24 and 25, '...through the redemption that is in Christ Jesus, *whom God set forth to be a propitiation*'. In all other religions, man has to find and provide his own sacrifice, but in the Christian faith it is God – the one who is offended! – who provides the atonement. The God who demands atonement is the very one who provides the atonement that will satisfy himself. God, in his great love and grace, has proceeded to accomplish this. In order to remain just and, at the same time, to justify the ungodly, he must satisfy the law, satisfy his own character and justice. 'Therefore,' declares God, 'who, other than myself, is able to make atonement? I shall do it. I shall provide my own Son as an atonement for sin.' It is the God of love who is at work here – the God of grace providing a way of satisfying the demands of his own justice in order to save sinners like you and me. The transgressor will be released, pronounced not guilty and justified, because of the atoning death of Jesus Christ upon the cross. God has set forth his Son as an atonement.

Cosmic child abuse?

At this point we meet another objection to the doctrine. This, it is said, is 'cosmic child abuse' – an angry, tyrannical Father torturing his Son in order to redeem sinners. What have we to say to this? We must first remember that Jesus Christ declared, 'I and my Father are one' (John 10:30). Just as the Father's heart beats with grace and love, so, to exactly the same degree and not one jot less, beats the Son's heart with grace and love. They are of one mind – like Father, like Son. The two are one in all their purposes and intentions towards sinners. This is the Holy Trinity – Three in One. They are one in purpose, one in nature, one in everything – and one in their love towards us. Whatever was at work when Christ was dying on the cross, it was certainly not because he did not love those sinners for whom he was dying. To use the word 'abuse' in such a context is wholly alien to the circumstances.

But, of course, the thing that puts an end to this red herring of 'cosmic child abuse' is that Christ went voluntarily to the cross. We could turn to a host of Scriptures that prove the point that he did not approach the cross under compulsion, and many of our hymns take up this theme, emphasising the readiness with which he undertook his work:

With pitying eyes, the Prince of grace
Beheld our helpless grief;
He saw, and, O amazing love!
He flew to our relief.

Down from the shining seats above,
With joyful haste He fled;
Entered the grave in mortal flesh,
And dwelt among the dead.

Isaac Watts (1674–1748)

If we turn to Paul's letter to the Philippians, we find these words concerning the Son: 'Who, being in the form of God, did not consider it robbery to be equal with God, but made himself of no reputation' (Phil. 2:6–7). Christ was not compelled to be of no reputation; he made himself of no reputation. He acted voluntarily; he 'made himself of no reputation, taking the form of a servant, and coming in the likeness of men'. He made himself nothing by adding humanity to his deity. And what happened next? 'And being found in appearance as a man, he humbled himself' (Phil. 2:8). He was not forced into humiliation – he humbled himself. He did all this voluntarily, becoming 'obedient to the point of death, even the death of the cross'. There is not the slightest shadow of a suggestion that he was being forced. God was not compelling him into doing something that he himself did not wish.

44

Consider the Trinity again. According to the hymn-writer,

> *Salvation's way for sinners lost, undone,*
> *Was counselled forth by God the Three in One.*

Peter Jones (1775–1845);
tr. by Edmund Tudor Owen (b. 1935)

It was not that the Father stated his mind, and the others had to submit. No! This was the counsel of the Three in One. God the Father loved the world so much that he gave his only begotten Son. And the Son described his own love in this way: 'This is my commandment, that you love one another as I have loved you. Greater love has no one than this, to lay down his life for his friends' (John 15:12–13). The two are agreed, Father and Son; there is no shade of difference. The 'cosmic child abuse' is buried for ever! And according to the letter to the Philippians, 'Therefore God also has highly exalted him and given him the name which is above every name' – you hardly do this to one whom you have tortured and abused! – 'that at the name of Jesus every knee should bow, of those in heaven, and of those on earth, and of those under the earth, and that every tongue should confess that Jesus Christ is Lord, to the glory of God the Father' (Phil. 2:9–11). Every step of the way, the Son is one hundred per cent involved.

The sufferings of Christ

We need to ask one further question. What did it mean for Jesus Christ to be made an atonement for his people? What did he have to endure before it could be said,

> *The Law's full consummation,*
> *A Father's approbation,*
> *Hear Zion's acclamation!*
> *In His blood.*

William Williams (1801–76);
tr. by William Vernon Higham (b. 1926).

Paul gives us the answer – 'through the redemption' (verse 24).

There was a price to pay and a suffering to endure. And we must endeavour, as far as we are able, to comprehend the price that was paid, and the depths of suffering that Jesus Christ had to undergo in order to make atonement.

Firstly, there was the *physical* suffering. We are familiar with the facts: the scourging, the spitting, the crown of thorns, the carrying of the cross; then the act of nailing the body upon the cross and lifting it up, and his hanging upon it for hours until death. And this is the problem. We are so familiar with the history that we can read it without being moved or much affected.

It would be better if we paused to consider what crucifixion during Roman times truly involved. It is impossible to imagine a more painfully drawn-out, excruciating and horrific death than crucifixion. We speak of 'terrorism'. The Romans understood this concept well enough. They had no wish to see hordes of thieves, murderers and rebels at large in their conquered lands. Their deterrent was crucifixion, and it was a terrifying one. When Jesus was carrying his cross, he was not being taken from the court of Pilate to Calvary by the shortest route, but toiling, step by step, through many of the streets of Jerusalem, precisely in order that all might see him. The purpose of this was to drive home the lesson: see what will happen to you if you break the law!

One commentator has described what happens physically during the process of crucifixion. The more you try to lessen your pain, the worse, in fact, the torture becomes. As you hang on the cross, it is hard to breathe; the lungs are constrained and compressed, and to fight for breath you must raise yourself up on the nails; but this only produces more pain. Then, breathing now more freely, you lower your torso in order to ease the pain, only to initiate the whole excruciating cycle again. I did not see Mel Gibson's film, *The Passion of Christ*, but I understand that it portrays the physical suffering of Christ in a very realistic way. I know of some who did see the film and were deeply moved by the view of this physical element of his sufferings.

46

How much more!

But Mel Gibson could never portray the depths of the suffering truly involved. The physical pain, though so horrific, was in the context only superficial. Jesus Christ, as he went to the cross, was carrying our sins with all their consequences. Consider the effects of sin between men – the pain we cause one another as a result of our sins. People are unkind to us, and we are hurt. And we in turn hurt others. Isaiah tells us that when Jesus Christ died on the cross he carried our sorrows (Isaiah 53:4). Here is a deeper level of suffering. The hymn-writer says,

> *He took my sins and my sorrows,*
> *He made them His very own;*
> *He bore the burden to Calvary,*
> *And suffered and died alone.*

Charles Homer Gabriel (1856–1932)

There was not only physical suffering on the cross, but inner, psychological suffering. We all know something of the pain of hurt and sorrow. Here is Jesus Christ bearing the hurt of an innumerable throng of people.

But there is more here again. William Williams, Pantycelyn, describes how

> *The enormous load of human guilt*
> *Was on my Saviour laid.*

This is another effect of sin, the guilt that we feel when we transgress. When you have been at fault, or unkind, or underhanded, and you know very well what you have done, you can feel thoroughly miserable. It is possible for such a sense of guilt to completely incapacitate you. And that is on account of only one sin! What if you had to bear the weight of guilt of a dozen sins all at the same time? And what if one were bearing the guilt of innumerable sins? What measure of suffering would that involve? This is what Jesus Christ did: he bore our guilt – all of it! It is impossible to plumb these depths, or to have any idea of what was involved.

But there is still more. In the Old Testament we have the account of an occasion when Moses stood on a hill to intercede for the nation as they fought. He had two helpers, Joshua and Caleb, to hold up his arms. It is good when facing life's problems to have friends for support. But Jesus Christ had no help:

> *Thou, who once wast thus bereft,*
> *That Thine own might ne'er be left.*
>
> John Ellerton, 1826–93

His journey to the cross to bear the suffering was made in absolute loneliness. According to Matthew's account of the Garden of Gethsemane (Matthew 26), three disciples had accompanied him to pray. He distances himself a stone's throw from them. After a period of praying he returns to them and, finding them all asleep, says to Peter, 'Could you not watch with me one hour?' They were not able to support his arms even for an hour! And by the end of the chapter we find that all the disciples have fled. As he left Gethsemane he knew he would have to face the awful sufferings of the cross on his own. And as he hung from the nails, there was no help from heaven either. 'My God, my God, why have you forsaken me?' he cried out. His own Father has left him! Absolute isolation!

A reservoir of wrath
There is even more: one more step to take, and it is connected with the previous point. The storm of God's wrath, God's determined rejection of sin, was about to fall on him. By this God would be appeased. We have not yet sought to explain one phrase in our paragraph in Romans 3. We read: 'whom God set forth ... to demonstrate his righteousness, because in his forbearance God had passed over the sins that were previously committed'

48

(verse 25). This refers us back to the Old Testament period when the sins of a multitude of people were forgiven, but without their accounts being cleared in heaven. (There had been sacrifices throughout this period, it is true, but these were only shadows of the one sacrifice to come.) So, throughout the Old Testament age, there was a storing up of the Father's wrath against the sins of the Old Testament saints. Behind a great dam there was a reservoir of wrath gathering, increasing in volume with the passing of the years as the saints of old received forgiveness. But no one had appeared to pay the cheque yet.

Then, with Christ hanging upon the cross, the complete torrent of that wrath was poured out upon him.

> *On the Mount of Crucifixion*
> *Fountains opened deep and wide;*
> *Through the floodgates of God's mercy*
> *Flowed a vast and gracious tide.*

William Rees (1802–83);
tr. by William Edwards (1843–1929)

When we sing these words, we think of the grace and the love of God, but the picture is true also of his wrath. The time of God's forbearance comes to an end, the dam bursts, and his wrath pours out upon the Son. Love upon us, but wrath upon him – and wrath not only for the sins of the past, but for all the sins of the saints of the future, throughout the ages.

What is the suffering involved in enduring the wrath of the Father against sin? There is no possible way to answer that question fully, but we may offer some feeble shadow of an answer. Some of us may have a child's memory of a father telling us, 'You are not to do this.' We then proceed to do that very thing. The time comes when you have to approach your father and account for yourself. He is sitting perfectly quietly. It would be so much easier if he were shouting and giving you a row! But he sits there quietly, looking at you with eyes full of love. There is no need for him to say anything. You know perfectly well that you have transgressed and gone against his will; you have done something that has displeased and disappointed him. You know that what you have done deserves his righteous anger, in his complete rejection of the action that you took. How do you feel? Upon the cross Jesus Christ faced his Father. When the wrath of God is being poured out upon the Son, the Father looks upon the Son with eyes full of love and says, 'You are now bearing the sins of many. My fixed and unyielding rejection of those sins will now befall you.' How did the Son feel at this point?

> *Death and the curse were in our cup:*
> *O Christ, 'twas full for Thee!*
> *But Thou hast drained the last dark drop,*
> *'Tis empty now for me:*
> *That bitter cup, love drank it up,*
> *Now blessing's draught for me.*

Anne Ross Cousin (1824–1906)

How long?
It took time to drink the dregs of that cup to the bitter end. How much time? Let me change the illustration and speak of computers. You know how you can download a computer programme or file. At the beginning of the download a sign appears on the screen, saying, for example, '8 minutes remaining'; you may know to the second how long you have to wait for the process to be completed.

When Christ's sufferings on the cross began, how many minutes lay ahead of him? Have you thought of that before? Would one minute be sufficient to download all that wrath? Would five minutes be necessary in order to receive the full wrath of the Father? One thing Jesus Christ knew: his suffering would not last for ever; he knew he would go to the Father; he knew the end of the story. But he did not know how long he would have to endure, how long would be the darkness before him. Did he know that it would take three hours? Why were three hours necessary? Would not two hours be sufficient? On the cross Jesus Christ bears the punishment of sin, minute after minute after minute. The first hour passes and he remains there still, groaning in spirit. The second hour passes, and then the third, and Jesus cries out, 'My God, why have you forsaken me?' He is quoting from Psalm 22.

What do we find in that psalm? Does it only give expression to a sense of God having departed? No, there are other aspects too, expressions of prayer and of the hope of salvation. The psalm that begins with the cry,

> My God, my God, why have you forsaken me?
> Why are you so far from helping me,
> And from the words of my groaning?

proceeds in verse 15 with the words,

> My strength is dried up like a potsherd,
> And my tongue clings to my jaws;
> You have brought me to the dust of death.
> For dogs have surrounded me;
> The assembly of the wicked has enclosed me.
> They pierced my hands and my feet;
> I can count all my bones.
> They look and stare at me.
> They divide my garments among them,
> And for my clothing they cast lots.
> But you, O LORD, do not be far from me;
> O my strength, hasten to help me!
> Deliver me from the sword...
>
> (verses 15–20)

So, after three hours, Christ is calling on his Father to release him! And his prayer was answered immediately. Within seconds of that cry came another, 'It is finished'. Why? Because the

Father responded to his Son's cry, 'Why have you forsaken me? Why is this continuing?' Suddenly the Father declares, 'I am satisfied!' And the moment he heard that declaration, the Son knew that all was accomplished.

> *Finished all the types and shadows*
> *Of the ceremonial law,*
> *Finished all that God had promised:*
> *Death and hell no more shall awe.*
> *'It is finished!'*
> *Saints the dying words record.*

Jonathan Evans (1749–1809)

There was no need to suffer further. The work was finished. Atonement for sin had been made. He could now say, 'Father, into your hands I commend my spirit.' The God-Man proceeds to his rest, to wait three days until the glorious day of his presentation to the world as the victorious One – the One who fulfilled all the demands of the Law. And his triumphant resurrection on the morning of the third day proclaimed his victory.

We have seen that God's law accuses every man of his sin, so that God stops every mouth. Silence is also the only appropriate response as we think of the atonement of Calvary and the suffering on the cross that brings all the blessings of heaven to the believer. As Williams, Pantycelyn, confessed in a Welsh hymn:

> *Rich blessings upon blessings,*
> *The fruits of Calvary,*
> *Sweet Eshcol grapes unnumbered,*
> *Maturing on that tree;*
> *As all of these surround me,*
> *How infinite their sum!*
> *I find myself amongst them,*
> *In deepest awe, struck dumb.*

4.

'Justification by faith'

'But now the righteousness of God...is revealed...
even the righteousness of God which is through
faith in Jesus Christ to all...
who believe'
(Romans 3: 21, 22)

Let me summarise the main points of the discussion so far. We have looked at the dark picture: 'for all have sinned and fall short of the glory of God' (Romans 3:23). We attended the law courts and were all of us found guilty. As Paul stated earlier in the chapter, 'that every mouth may be stopped, and all the world may become guilty before God' (verse 19). Every one of us is under the wrath and judgement of God.

We then proceeded to discuss what it was that God did to meet the need of mankind in this wretched condition. We again visited the law courts and saw that on the Last Day God declares an innumerable number of people not guilty, and that he justifies them. God justifies the ungodly! We also saw why he does this. It is because of his love and grace: 'being justified freely, by his grace' (verse 24). We then considered the problem of how a just God could justify the ungodly. The answer of the Scriptures is that God can remain just, and yet justify, 'through the redemption that is in Christ Jesus, whom God set forth to be a propitiation' (verse 24, 25). And so we dwelt upon this One who gave himself as an atonement for our sins, to deliver us from what we deserved and to ensure our salvation. And we considered also the suffering that was bound up in such a work.

Before continuing we should look, in passing, at another important point. We say that Christ's death was a vicarious, or substitutionary, death. What is the meaning of the word 'substitutionary'? We are familiar with the use of the term on the sports field. The substitute is the one who takes the place of another who was on the field before him. And this is how we are to understand the death of Jesus Christ: he died a substitutionary death. As he died on the cross, Jesus Christ was taking our place.

This is perfectly evident in the Scriptures. 'But God demonstrates his own love towards us, in that while we were still sinners, Christ died for us' (Romans 5:8). He died *'for us'*, or in our place. Again, 'who gave himself for our sins, that he might deliver us from this present evil age' (Galatians 1:4). It was a substitutionary death, but it was also a substitutionary atonement, and a substitutionary punishment (penal substitution). That is, Jesus Christ, because of his great love, bore and suffered what we deserved, and the result, as we have seen, was great suffering for him.

Declared 'not guilty'

Let us now proceed further. To illustrate the work of Jesus Christ on the cross, paying the price for us so that we might be released, we related what happened with *Cymdeithas yr Iaith Gymraeg* (the Welsh Language Society) and the law courts of the sixties, when others paid the fines for the poor students to secure their release, If, however, you were to delve into the legal archives, you would find that the names of those students are still on the books as guilty individuals. Were they to transgress again, someone would be returning to look up those archives and announce that they had a 'record'. They had been found guilty of breaking the law and had been pronounced guilty, but they were released because others paid their fine.

The doctrine of justification involves so much more than the bearing of another's punishment. What occurs at the Day of Judgement is not that God declares, 'These are guilty, but Jesus Christ has paid the price', but rather, 'These are not guilty.' That is the nature of justification. To justify is to do more than forgive sins; it is the declaration that the guilty are not guilty. This is exactly what Paul is telling us when he says, 'the righteousness of God…is revealed', and it is 'the righteousness of God which is through faith in Jesus Christ to all…who believe' (verses 21, 22). He is not simply saying that there is forgiveness of sins to all who believe. No, his emphasis here is on the righteousness of God to all who believe. It is not only that our sins are accounted to Jesus Christ, but also that his righteousness is made over to our account. His righteousness – the fruit of that perfect life which he lived on earth in complete obedience to his Father – is accounted to us.

Clothed in his righteousness

This is clear from the paragraph we are considering – 'the righteousness of God…is revealed' (verse 21) – and also from many other verses of Scripture. For example, Romans 4:6 speaks of 'the blessedness of the man to whom God imputes righteousness'; Romans 5:17 refers to those 'who receive…the gift of righteousness'; 1 Corinthians 1:30 describes Christ Jesus as one who 'became for us…righteousness', and in Philippians 3:9 Paul rejoices at 'being found in him, not having my own righteousness…but that which is through faith in Christ, the righteousness which is from God by faith'. It amounts to this: there is more to salvation than the forgiveness of sins; there is also this great, wonderful dimension of righteousness being accounted to us.

Imagine two brothers. One of them has made shipwreck of his life and is in great debt. The other has had remarkable success and become a multi-millionaire. The day arrives when the debtor approaches his brother and confesses he is in trouble. His debts are enormous; is there any possibility of his brother being willing to clear them? Imagine the wealthy brother saying, 'No problem! I'll write a cheque for you now to cover them all.' That would mean that the first brother's bank account would be out of the red and, with no debts, he could make a new start. If that were the wealthy brother's response, we would all commend him for his generosity. But imagine this! When the brothers meet, the rich man tells the poor man, 'Look here, why don't we exchange bank accounts? I'll take your account with all its debts, and I'll give you mine with all its millions.' It is this second picture that conveys something of the meaning of justification.

For a scriptural picture we turn to Isaiah 61:10 – 'He has clothed me with the garments of salvation, he has covered me with the robe of righteousness.' The dirty rags are taken away by the Lord Jesus Christ, but instead of leaving us naked he clothes the sinner with the robes of righteousness. When clothed in these, the sinner is not guilty in God's sight; God's righteousness has been accounted to him.

Is it possible for a person who has been justified in this way to sin? Yes, certainly it is. After our conversion we are still in the flesh. Temptations will arise and we will still fall into sin, unfortunately – not completely as before, it is true, for the process of sanctification is active in our lives. But what we are considering now is not the believer's condition, but his status. Our status is eternally secure from the very beginning, because we are clothed in the righteousness of the Lord Jesus Christ. And when we shall appear at the Judgement Day, it will not be our sins that God sees, but the robe, the righteousness of his Son. Charles Wesley sings:

> *Accepted in the Well-beloved,*
> *And clothed in righteousness divine,*
> *I see the bar to heaven removed,*
> *And all Thy merits, Lord, are mine.*

The only hope of the sinner at the Last Day is that he or she will be one of those who will hear the Father say, 'Not guilty'. Are you one of these people? Are you sure that you are one of them? We saw in *Pilgrim's Progress* the picture of two people travelling to the Celestial City without entering through the wicket gate. They had not experienced conviction of sin nor found relief at the foot of the cross, but had come into the narrow way by jumping over a wall. Their names were Formality and Hypocrisy. Are you one of those? Or will you, on that dreadful day, be found amongst those who are justified 'through the redemption that is in Christ Jesus, whom God set forth to be a propitiation'?

'Through faith'

Who are these people, this innumerable host, that are pronounced not guilty by virtue of Jesus Christ's atoning work? In the paragraph of Scripture we are considering Paul tells us three times who they are. He speaks first of 'the righteousness of God which is through *faith* in Jesus Christ to all and on all who believe' (verse 22); then, later on, 'through *faith*' (verse 25), and 'the justifier of the one who has *faith* in Jesus' (verse 26). Those who will hear the pronouncement 'Not guilty' on the Day of Judgement are the people who have this faith. We are justified through faith. The connection between the sinner and this estate of being clothed in the righteousness of Jesus Christ is *faith*.

What is faith? The essence of faith is to believe something. In the Bible, faith is to believe God, *to take God at his word and act accordingly*. That is the first step.

In everyday life we all exercise faith at one level. When walking down the street, for example, we may come to a manhole cover, and we will step onto it quite happily and continue on our way. (In a comedy film, of course, the cover would collapse, followed by the inevitable fall into the hole.) In placing your foot on the cover you are exercising faith. You assume that the workman who placed it there did his job properly, that the cover itself is sound and that it can hold your weight. You have believed in man, you have trusted in Town Council workers. Everyone has to exercise faith at a certain level; otherwise it would be impossible to live. But God himself declares, 'Believe in me'. We believe one another in a hundred and one things, and if we can believe fallen, mortal men and act on their words, how much more should we believe God! He says to us, 'I tell you that the way to salvation is to believe in the Lord Jesus Christ who died for sinners on the cross.' Believe God.

If you read the commentaries, they will explain that there are three elements to this faith, and that the three are presented to us in the Scriptures continually. Firstly, there is the element of knowledge. You cannot gain faith unless you first know something. By now, we have obtained knowledge: we heard that God is holy and that we are sinners and come short of his glory; we have been reminded that the wrath of God is revealed from heaven against all ungodliness and unrighteousness; we saw that God justifies the ungodly and that he does so through the redemption obtained at the cross of Calvary. That is the knowledge.

The second step is to be convinced that this knowledge is true. To be able to say, 'Yes, this is not a theory. It's not a myth or a fairy tale. This is reality. I am a sinner; there is a God; there is wrath, and there is the death of Jesus Christ on the cross.' You know it is all true. The Holy Spirit has illuminated your mind, and the truth sweeps over you like a wave. But you are not a Christian yet. According to the Scriptures, the evil spirits know that the gospel is true, as does the Evil One himself!

So the third step, the third element of faith, is the step of trust: that moment when you place your foot on the manhole cover, knowing that it will hold your weight; that moment when you step into the aeroplane, knowing that you will soon be in the air; that moment when you dive into the swimming pool and trust to the water to hold up your body. It is that moment of reflection and of deciding, 'Yes, I believe. I will now act on the basis of your word, O God. I accept that Jesus Christ is a Saviour, and a Saviour for me.'

The well-known lines of a hymn express it beautifully,

> *I came to Jesus as I was,*
> *Weary, and worn, and sad;*
> *I found in him a resting-place,*
> *And He has made me glad.*

Horatius Bonar (1808–89)

You know the facts, you are convicted of their truth, and a moment comes when you rest and believe. That is the point when

the saving relationship with Jesus Christ begins. Any other previous relationship with Christ is insufficient.

'Jesus Christ and him crucified'

When evangelising, we are not to call on people to come to
Christ, and that alone. Unitarians may do that; they may call people to come to Jesus as a good man. The liberal theologians of
the last century would call people to come to Jesus because he
was an example of how we ought to live. The Muslims have a
respect for Jesus as a prophet. Therefore, we do not call people
to Jesus as a good man, though there has never been a better. It
is not enough even to call people to Jesus Christ, the Son of God.
The Roman Catholics are thoroughly orthodox in their doctrine
of the Person of the Son but, as is well known, the doctrine
of justification by faith does not belong to the teachings of that
Church.

   No, like Paul, we are to preach 'Jesus Christ and him crucified'
(1 Corinthians 2:2). We do not call people to the person only, but
to the person and to what he did, the work he came into the world
to accomplish. People must be brought to the foot of the cross,
where they will meet the Saviour. (To come any other way is to
come over the wall.) The initial relationship with the Lord Jesus
Christ is the viewing of him as a Saviour. It is from that initial
sight that the view of him as Shepherd, Friend, Brother, and
every other image of Christ will emerge. We begin at the foot of
the cross, with the Saviour becoming the Lord of our lives.

   Have we been there? Are you there presently? Forget about the
past – perhaps some of you are looking back and are unsure as
to when or how you became Christians. Are you at the
cross now?

> *Just as I am, without one plea,*
> *But that Thy blood was shed for me,*
> *And that Thou bidd'st me come to Thee,*
> *O Lamb of God, I come.*

Charlotte Elliott (1789–1871)

This is the call of the gospel. 'Come to me, all you who labour and are heavy laden' under the burden of sin. The invitation comes from Christ, dying on the cross. Bunyan describes his Pilgrim arriving at the foot of the cross, and looking, and looking, and looking. His burden falls away and his tears begin to flow. He realises that salvation has been given him. One look of faith at the sacrifice of the cross brings us into a saving relationship with the Lord Jesus Christ. He, now, is our Saviour.

There is nothing for us to do

This faith, therefore, through which we are justified, requires that we take God at his word and act accordingly. The second thing that may be said about it is that it is contrary to every desire and attempt to help ourselves. This is a problem to many people. In spite of everything that has been said, there may still be someone saying, 'I will now go home to read a chapter of the Bible. I will now go home to pray. I will go home and endeavour to be more faithful in my attendance at church. I will go home to do some good work.' There is something in us that always wants to *do* something.

But God is determined that we must get it into our heads that there is nothing for us to do. Faith is the answer. As far as salvation is concerned, faith is opposed to works. The essence of this faith is that you yield, confessing there is nothing you can do; you have reached an end of yourself and are unable to do anything. The essence of this faith is to say to God that he must do everything, and to believe that he did do everything when Jesus Christ died on the cross for us.

> *Nothing in my hand I bring,*
> *Simply to Thy cross I cling;*
> *Naked, come to Thee for dress,*
> *Helpless, look to Thee for grace.*

Augustus Montague Toplady (1740–78)

Faith in Jesus Christ! Have you come to that place? Perhaps you have followed everything up to this point. You have come to understand things, and have been convicted that they are true, and now you are asking how you may be one of that innumerable band that shall be pronounced not guilty on the Last Day. The Scriptures say that you may be justified through faith in the redemption. You must say, 'I come.'

Rejoicing

It is at this point that the glorying begins. 'In the cross of Christ I glory,' says the hymn. You cannot glory until you have passed through conviction of sin, have come to the foot of the cross, and have felt the burden fall off your back. Notice Isaiah 61:10. The verse begins, 'I will greatly rejoice in the Lord, my soul shall be joyful in my God.' Why? Because 'he has clothed me with the garments of salvation, he has covered me with the robe of righteousness.' Isaiah rejoices because he knows he has been justified. What of the apostle Peter? 'Now... believing, you rejoice with joy inexpressible and full of glory, receiving the end of your faith – the salvation of your souls' (1 Peter 1:8,9).

When does the rejoicing begin? As you believe. At the moment of repentance – which may be an experience full of torment – that is when the glory and joy begin. Again it is the hymn-writer who expresses this so well. A translation of a Welsh hymn begins,

> *There is a path of pardon*
> *In his blood;*

and the second verse runs,

> *O come, ye sons of Adam,*
> *And rejoice!*
> *Now trust the God of Abraham*
> *And rejoice!*
> *O hasten, happy sinner,*
> *To life in Christ for ever,*

To bonds that naught can sever:
O rejoice!
In full and glad surrender
Come, rejoice!

William Williams (1801–76);
tr. by William Vernon Higham (b. 1926)

These old hymn-writers knew their theology. They understood justification by faith. They understood the Scriptures and expressed their truths wonderfully. Have you come to faith? Do you rejoice?

But here again we have a problem. We who believe are now in the faith, and yet very often our rejoicing is not what it should be. We experience tiredness and weariness. Our view of these great truths can become dull. A cloud covers them and discouragement creeps over us, and the joy that should be in us as a result of our faith in Christ often evaporates. We go to church sometimes on a Sunday morning, the Day of Resurrection, and instead of praising and rejoicing in God we are heavy and slow. There is a great weakness in the flesh.

But a day will come when we shall leave this tabernacle and shall enter into the eternal glory of heaven. We shall join the heavenly choir.

Then in a nobler, sweeter song
I'll sing Thy power to save,
When this poor lisping, stammering tongue
Lies silent in the grave.

William Cowper (1731–1800)

This is pictured for us in the fifth chapter of the Book of Revelation. Those who have faith in Jesus Christ will be declared not guilty by the great Judge on the Day of Judgement. We will enter heaven, and sing the new song:

'You are worthy to take the scroll, and to open its seals;

for you were slain, and have redeemed us to God by your blood out of every tribe and tongue and people and nation.'

We shall sing it because we have known of that experience:

'You…have made us kings and priests to our God; and we shall reign on the earth.'

We shall delight to add our voice to the singing of the anthems.

Then I looked, and I heard the voice of many angels around the throne, the living creatures, and the elders; and the number of them was ten thousand times ten thousand, and thousands of thousands, saying with a loud voice: 'Worthy is the Lamb who was slain to receive power and riches and wisdom, and strength and honour and glory and blessing.'

I shall rejoice in God my salvation. I shall glory in the cross of Christ!

And every creature which is in heaven and on earth and under the earth and such as are in the sea, and all that are in them, I heard saying: 'Blessing and honour and glory and power be to him who sits on the throne, and to the Lamb, for ever and ever!' Then the four living creatures said, "Amen."'

He will keep me till the river
Rolls its waters at my feet:
Then He'll bear me safely over,
Where the loved ones I shall meet.
Yes, I'll sing the wondrous story
Of the Christ who died for me;
Sing it with the saints in glory,
Gathered by the crystal sea.

Francis Harold Rawley (1854–1952)

Postscript

This book leads us to the very heart of historic Christianity. The Glory of the Cross is understood when we see that the impaled and immolated Christ is not simply helpless victim, rather that the Cross was the instrument by which our Lord wielded his Almightiness, through the Eternal Spirit, as the weapon of his warfare so that it became the means of his victory over sin, Satan and death. Christ was not simply suffering the will of God, he was doing it.

The Cross was not the stake of a martyr: it was a theatre of war, the scene of a mighty conflict. Incalculable spiritual power was being wielded. Sin was being rendered impotent; death was being destroyed; the rulers of the darkness of this world were being routed. At no point of our Lord's death was there loss of consciousness or exhaustion of strength. His spirit is not simply to depart, or to expire. It is rather dismissed, on the authority of the Saviour, as a magnificent shout of triumph reverberates through heaven, earth and hell – 'It is finished!' So forgiveness in the Bible is grounded firmly in the rectitude of God, not his indulgence. It is a righteous act, and a judicial action sanctioned by the Moral law. The sacrifice of the Lord of glory, the blood of God the Son, justify justification. In the flesh of the Son of God the sins of the church of God have been condemned.

Therefore, in the logic of redemption, there is now no condemnation. In Christ, they are all that the righteousness of God requires the Holy One to require, and for that reason not only may God forgive them, but God may not forgive them. It is to the divine fidelity that the eloquence of the Cross is ultimately addressed. Who is he that condemns? It is Christ Jesus that died. That is the Glory of the Cross.

Geoff Thomas
Alfred Place Baptist Church, Aberystwyth